Mind Maps®
for kids

Mind Maps® for kids

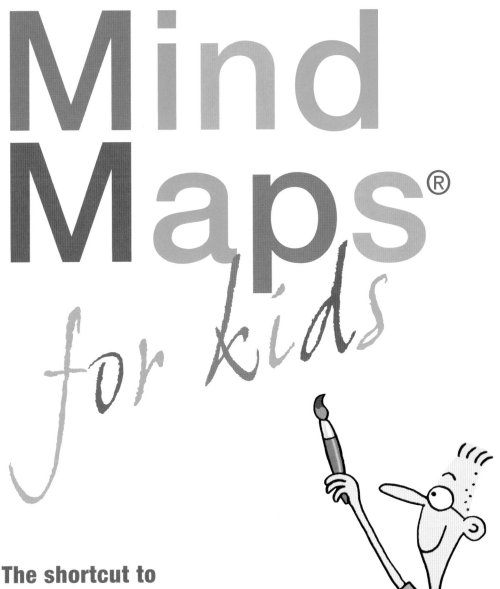

The shortcut to success at school

Tony Buzan

With additional material from
Zoe Barry-Hughes BSc (London), PGCE (North London)

Mind Map® is a registered trademark of The Buzan Organisation.

HarperThorsons
An Imprint of HarperCollins*Publishers*
77–85 Fulham Palace Road,
Hammersmith, London W6 8JB

The Thorsons website address is: www.thorsonselement.com

and *HarperThorsons* are trademarks
of HarperCollins*Publishers* Limited

First published by Thorsons 2003

12

A catalogue record of this book
is available from the British Library

ISBN-10 0-00-715133-0
ISBN-13 978-0-00-715133-2

Cartoons and Mind Map® illustrations by Martin Shovel

Printed and bound in Great Britain
by Butler Tanner and Dennis, Frome, Somerset

Dedication

Mind Maps® for Kids is dedicated to kids everywhere: to their amazing minds and their boundless creativity.

Especially to 'The Mind Map Kids' who helped me: Edmund Trevelyan-Johnson; Alexander Keene; Alex Brandis; Michael Collins; the children of Berryhill School in Scotland; the children of Willow Run School in Detroit; the children in Singapore's Learning and Thinking Schools; the children of Seabrook Primary School in Australia; and, finally, to 'Mind Map Kids' everywhere!

Acknowledgments

With special thanks to my Mind Maps for Kids Supporters Team at Thorsons: Helen Evans, my Editor, for her dedication and commitment in bringing this project together; Carol Tonkinson (and her new kid!), my Commissioning Editor; Jacqueline Burns, my Acting Editor-in-Chief; Megan Slyfield, my Publicity Director; and the leader of the team, Belinda Budge.

Special thanks also to the wonderful Design Team: Jo Ridgeway, Design Manager; Natasha Fidler, for her genius book design; Sonia Dobie, Cover Design Manager; and to Nicole Linhardt, my Production Controller. Thanks also to Zoe Barry-Hughes for her wonderful input and enthusiastic support, and to Caroline Shott, my Literary Manager, who made this dream come true.

Special thanks also to my Mind Maps for Kids Home Team: Lesley Bias for her 'flying fingers'; and to Vanda North for introducing kids around the world to the magic of Mind Maps.

Contents

Letter from

Homework. Yuk! When faced with it, do you, like I did, find yourself putting it off with **brilliant excuses** like phoning friends, watching television, playing computer games and reading magazines until the time has run out? And **of course** you will always do it tomorrow ... Yeah, yeah, yeah!

Do you, like I did, worry about tests or exams?

Do you, like I did, ever daydream about a **magic tool** that would make homework easy, that would help you pass exams, ace tests, surprise your teachers, impress your friends and amaze examiners? Would you like some **secret formula** that would help you concentrate and which would zap your schoolwork into something that took nanoseconds, while making your free time stretch off into infinity – and beyond!

If only ...

I travelled around the world investigating and making exciting discoveries about our brains and how they really work and what they really need to help make them work better. Eventually I discovered that secret formula. In actual fact I had to invent it! That secret formula is called the **Mind Map**®.

Mind Maps have helped me to write, solve problems and make my life easier and more successful. They can do the same for you. Mind Maps have already helped millions of students around the world get **better grades** with **less work**. Mind Maps can bring about success.

In this book I will show you how you can arm yourself with the ultimate classroom secret formula, using no more than a few coloured pens – and your brain.

'But how?' I hear you ask. 'Surely the contents of my pencil case can't be that powerful?'

Ahhhhh, when used alongside your amazing brain, it can.

And you are about to find out how ...

TONY BUZAN

How to Mind Map®

Imagine a **shortcut** that could help to cut your homework time in half and to have more **fun**.

Welcome to the wonderf

Imagine a **magic formula** that could help you to get started and **do well** on any project.

Imagine a **secret method** for making it easy to come up with ideas, easy to **solve problems** and easy to remember things.

world of the Mind Map!

What is a Mind Map?

★ A Mind Map is an easy way to get information into and out of your brain.

★ A Mind Map is a new way of studying and revising that is quick and works.

★ A Mind Map is a way of taking notes that is not boring.

★ A Mind Map is the best way of coming up with new ideas and planning projects.

A Mind Map is made up of **words**, **colours**, **lines** and **pictures**. It is very easy to construct. Mind Maps can help you to:

★ Remember better
★ Come up with brilliant ideas
★ Save time and make the most of the time you have
★ Get better grades
★ Organize your thinking, your hobbies and your life
★ Have more fun!

A Mind Map is your secret formula!

Why do Mind Maps Work?

What do you think is the most common word used by students around the world to describe note-taking?

You're correct: **BORING!** To find out why, do the following little quiz.

When you are taking notes do you:

1. Write them along lines? — YES/NO
2. Write in one colour — especially blue or black ink? — YES/NO
3. Sometimes have lists in your notes? — YES/NO
4. Find that all the words blend into each other instead of jumping out at you? — YES/NO
5. Find that every page looks the same? — YES/NO

If you answered 'YES' to most of these questions, you are like 99% of the world's student note-takers. And, like you, they also find their notes boring!

Let's look at what your brain needs in order to make note-taking fascinating.

Have a good look at the **functions** of each side of your brain. When you are making notes at school or doing homework, **which side of your brain** do you think you usually use the most?

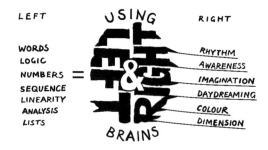

The answer is probably 'left', isn't it?

This is probably because:

- ★ *You use lined paper*
- ★ *You make notes in lists*
- ★ *The main item in your notes will be words*
- ★ *You use numbers to structure the order of your words*
- ★ *You try to be logical in what you do*
- ★ *Your classroom desks are often organized in lines*
- ★ *When desperately trying to remember, if you are like most students, you try to remember the words and numbers.*

These are all left-brain skills. This means you use only **half of your brain's amazing potential** when you make standard notes.

Concentration

Mind Maps keep you focussed on the main idea and all the additional ideas. They help you use both sides of your brain so that it actually becomes difficult to tear yourself away from your studies.

Mind Maps for Kids

Your brain thinks in **colours** and **pictures** – and I can prove it.

Say, for instance, I said to you, '**Your house**', what would pop into your head? Would it be a computer printout of the word, written in a line across the page, or would you get a **picture in your mind** of your house, the bricks, the doors, the windows?

Do you see what I mean? It was the **picture of your house in colour** that came into your mind first and not the words written on a piece of paper.

Your brain thinks and remembers in pictures. You already know how natural and easy this is by the way in which pictures in your photograph albums, books or magazines immediately bring back your memories. So, if you want to **remember** your house, or anything else, the best way to do it is to **draw a picture** of it.

Imagine you are moving house and you are not happy about it. You love your home and you want to remember it for ever, but you are worried that you will forget what it was like. If you were taking notes the normal way, you might write a list of all the rooms in your house, like this.

Mum and Dad's bedroom	Living room
My bedroom	Kitchen
Spare room	Bathroom

You would try and memorize the words in the form of a list and store it in your brain that way. Knowing now, as you do, that your brain thinks in pictures and colours, you could try a more brain-friendly method.

It's time to try a Mind Map.

How to Mind Map

As we saw earlier, the best way of reminding yourself of your house is to draw it, like this.

To remind yourself of all the different rooms, you could use **different coloured pens** to draw a separate line from the house for each room. Maybe you could use yellow to remind you of the kitchen, red for the lounge, and so on.

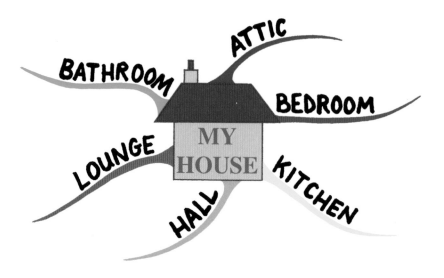

It doesn't really matter what colour you use; the colours are there to separate each item and to make the note more fun to do and easier to remember.

To make it clear what each branch coming from the house means, you would then label it with a different room. You could **add pictures** of each of the rooms, if you had time, to make it even easier to remember.

You have drawn a basic Mind Map.

How to Make a Mind Map

Making Mind Maps is easy. Just remember these **five easy steps:**

1. Use a blank sheet of unlined paper and some coloured pens. Make sure the paper is placed sideways.

2. Draw a picture in the middle of the page that sums up your main subject. The picture represents your main topic.

3. Draw some thick curved, connected lines coming away from the picture in the middle of the page, one for each of the main ideas you have about your subject. The central branches represent your main sub-topic.

4. Name each of these ideas and, if you want, draw a little picture of each – this uses both sides of the brain. Words are underlined throughout a Mind Map. This is because they are *key* words, and the underlining, as in normal notes, shows their importance.

5. From each of these ideas, you can draw other connected lines, spreading like the branches of a tree. Add your thoughts on each of these ideas. These additional branches represent the details.

The Mind Map Tool Kit

The Mind Map Tool Kit is very simple. It is so small you could carry it anywhere. In fact, there are very few tools needed at all. To **complete your first Mind Map** the only things you will need are:

★ Paper
★ Coloured pens
★ Your brain.

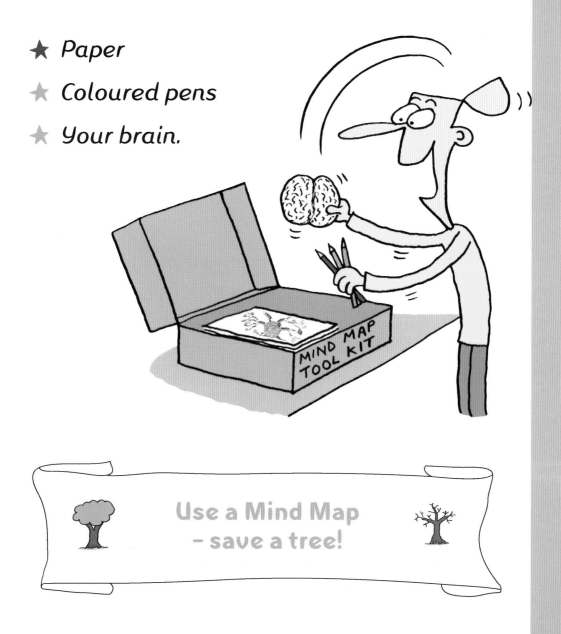

Use a Mind Map
– save a tree!

Mind Mapping Yourself

Have you got your **tool kit** together? Now you are ready to start your first Mind Map.

Below and opposite are two Mind Maps: one is already complete (below) for you to use as an example, the other (opposite) is blank for you to fill in by yourself. Take a good look at the first example before you begin, and feel free to use it as a guide while you make your own **Mind Map**.

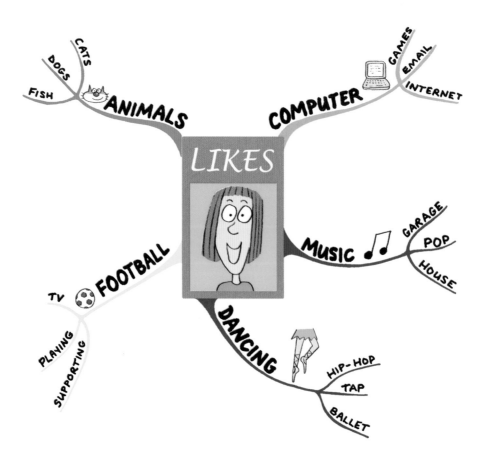

We are going to take an easy and very important subject, one on which you can boast of being a world expert: **You and your favourite things** – your 'likes'.

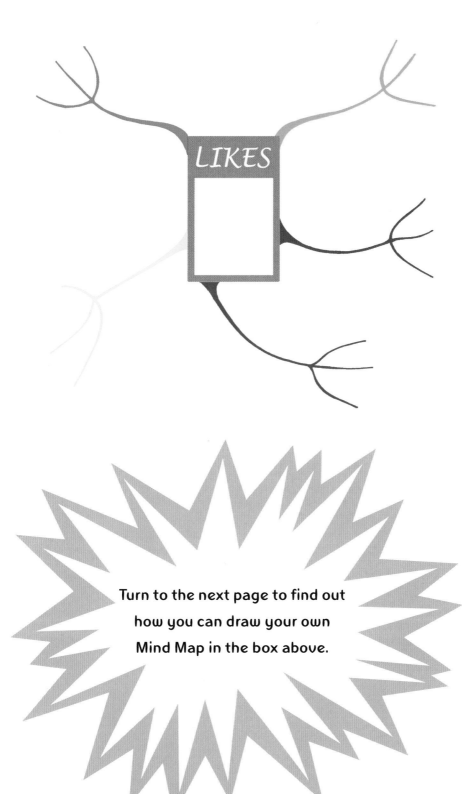

LIKES

Turn to the next page to find out
how you can draw your own
Mind Map in the box above.

In the middle of page 13 you will find a picture frame with the word 'Likes' at the top. Begin by **drawing a picture of yourself** in the picture frame underneath the word 'Likes'. It doesn't have to be a masterpiece; a quick sketch will do. Use your different coloured pens to colour in your hair and your eyes and, if you can, draw yourself wearing your favourite clothes.

Coming off the **central image** are **five octopus-like branches**, which have been drawn in already. On each one print in *big* and *bold* **letters**, one of the five things in the world you like the most (for instance, music, playing computer games, animals, football, dancing, etc.)

That was easy, wasn't it?

Go back and add **three new branches** off each of your five favourite 'Likes'. Add these new branches at the end or trigger point of your main branches. Make sure you connect them. These next branches are like the smaller branches or twigs coming off the main branches of a tree. Next, print in slightly smaller – but still clear – words the **three main things** you think of that go with each of your five main 'Likes'. For instance, if one of your 'likes' is music you might add the main types of music, or if one of your main likes is animals, then dogs, cats and fish.

That was easy, too, wasn't it?

In the pages that follow, you will see how this secret formula can put you one step (and sometimes miles!) ahead. You will see just how easy it really is.

Now think about it.

★ *Could you add more branches off the central image?*
  Of course you could.

★ *Could you add second level branches to all your main level branches?*
  Of course you could.

★ *Could you add at least two to three third level branches off the second level branches?*
  Of course you could!

★ *How long could you possibly go on adding branches?*
  Forever! The Mind Map has already helped you prove that your brain's capacity to think and come up with ideas is infinite.

Go back to the Mind Map on you and your likes and add anything else you want. When you have finished, **congratulate yourself**. You have just completed your first Mind Map.

You have 3 minutes on 'what you like...'

MASTER MIND (MAPPER!)

Chapter Two

What to do with Mind Maps®

In this chapter, you will start to see how Mind Maps can make your life **much easier** and **more fun**. They are the **ultimate secret formula** when it comes to:

★ Remembering things

★ Making better notes

★ Coming up with ideas

★ Saving time

★ Concentrating

★ Making the most of
   your time

★ Acing exams.

Maps do for you?

Remembering Things

Have you heard the one about ... oh, er, how does it go?

Have you ever started to tell a joke, only to find you can't remember how it goes? You know the answer is there in your head – somewhere!

Don't let it wind you up! A Mind Map is the **easiest way** of **getting the answers out of your head.** Yes, a Mind Map can help you remember corny jokes!

Look at the Mind Map on the facing page and see if you can come up with the punch line.

Memory
Think forgetting is a problem? Forget it! Mind Maps will help you forget you ever had a problem with memory!

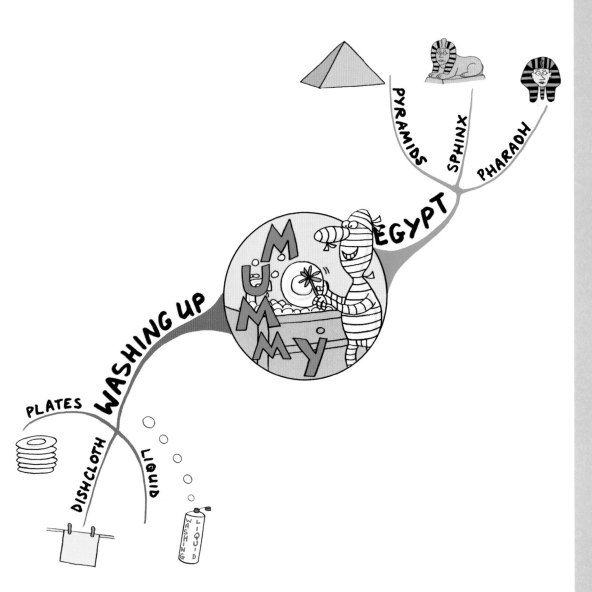

PYRAMIDS

SPHINX

PHARAOH

EGYPT

MUMMY

WASHING UP

PLATES

DISHCLOTH

LIQUID

WASHING LIQUID

You see how easy it is to get the things out of your head when you draw and write it all down. Mind Maps are the perfect way of **tracking down lost information**.

What do you call a mummy that washes up?

Pharaoh Liquid!

Making Notes

Remember, **your brain does not think just in straight lines**. That's why trying to memorize things for a test by reading and making lists of notes doesn't work, and you waste time by reading the same thing over and over again.

Look at the newspaper article on the opposite page. Imagine you have been given it to learn for a general knowledge quiz at school. Rather than just reading it through again and again, hoping that your poor brain will remember a little more each time, you are going to read though it just once.

While you are reading it, try to imagine that you will have to tell someone what it is about when you have finished. This helps to **focus your mind**.

You can help your brain to make connections by using the '**Question Kit**' on page 22. Ask these questions as you read the text and the answers will pop out for you, making **understanding**, **memory** and **Mind Mapping** much more easy.

CONQUERED

Harold is killed, Normans storm in and

England demands – how did it happen?

ENGLAND writhes under the heel of Europe today after being conquered by the Normans.

Our brave King Harold is dead – cut down as he tried to defend his realm against the massed ranks of the French invaders.

His brothers Earl Leofwine and Earl Gyrth and many elite house-carl troops also perished in the slaughter yesterday.

A triumphant Duke William of Normandy is already on his way from the battlefield near Hastings, Sussex, to London to seize the throne he claims is rightfully his. Sickeningly, he plans his coronation in Westminster Abbey on Christmas Day.

With the English army devastated, it is not expected that 38-year-old William – a cousin of 46-year-old King Harold's predecessor Edward the Confessor – will meet any resistance.

An inquiry has already been launched into how England, obsessed with the illegal immigration of Vikings in the North, lost a far more crucial battle against the Normans despite outnumbering them and commanding the best tactical position.

'When it came down to it, the English were just not good enough,' said one observer. 'They were brave, but they looked tired and were eventually hopelessly outmanoeuvred.'

The battle started at breakfast time yesterday and it seemed at first that the Norman army might be repulsed. But the 11,000-strong English force seemed bewildered by the wily enemy tactics.

Harold had picked what had seemed an impregnable stronghold along the Senlac ridge, from which to mount a classic defence beneath the normally all-conquering Anglo-Saxon shield-wall.

However, the 8,000 Normans had brought not only infantry, but archers and cavalrymen. Heralded by a blare of trumpets, the bowmen let fly. The infantrymen waded in and the cavalry picked off anything that was left.

'All we had were javelins, two-handed axes and stones tied to sticks,' said one English survivor. 'Our own knights never got going.'

Hopes that England would win rose amid rumours that William had been killed. Then the Norman leader appeared on horseback and English spirits wilted.

With foreign cunning, he pretended to be losing and sounded to retreat. But as soon as our infantry rushed after the Frenchmen, they were rounded on and massacred.

Even William had to salute the heroic last stand of the English. 'They stood firmly, as if fixed to the ground,' he said. 'The dead, by falling, seemed to move more than the living.'

Harold was buried in an unconsecrated grave. With him lay the hopes of his country.

By Orderic Vitalis
Warfare Chronicler
© Daily Mail

What to do with Mind Maps

Question Kit
Use this handy checkmap to help you.

MIND MAPPING AN ARTICLE

1. Use a blank sheet of paper and some coloured pens.

2. Pick out the main topic of the article and draw it in the centre of your page. This will summarize what the article is about – in this case, the Battle of Hastings. Be sure to make the image stand out. Colour it in! Colouring in always helps.

3. Draw some lines coming from your central picture. These will be for your sub-topics – the main elements that make up the story. Remember your What–Where–When–Who–Why checkmap to help you.

4. Fill in the details of this sub-topic level of facts. Use key images or key words printed clearly on the lines.

5. Next, draw some branches coming off each of the points so you can add a third, detailed, level of facts to your Mind Map. This is where you can fit in all those juicy little facts that are easy to forget in tests – dates, names or numbers, for example. You only need to use single words, a date or a number, not full sentences.

Tip: Use colours to make things stand out easily.

Now look at the Mind Map on the next page and see what differences there are in content from yours. They will be different, because a Mind Map is a map **out-side your** head of what is going on **inside your head**, and the thoughts in your head are unique. Your Mind Map will be as individual as you are.

KILLED

HAROLD

BURIED

THRONE

CORONATION WILLIAM

WESTMINSTER

CHRISTMAS

46 HAROLD ENGLISH

11,000

INFANTRY JAVELINS

STONES

AXES

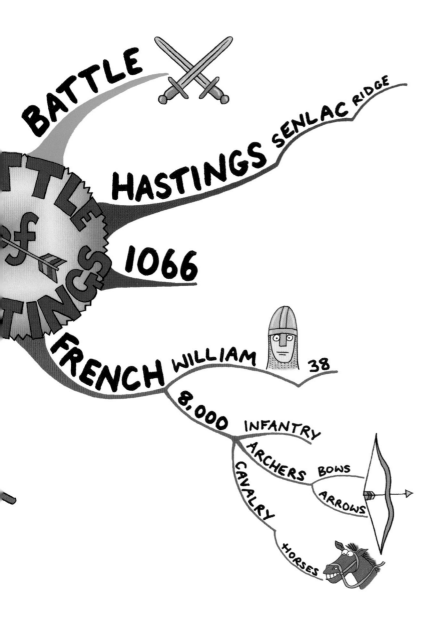

BATTLE

HASTINGS SENLAC RIDGE

BATTLE of HASTINGS

1066

FRENCH WILLIAM 38

8,000 INFANTRY

ARCHERS BOWS

ARROWS

CAVALRY

HORSES

Note Making
(taking notes from your own head)

Mind Maps help you 'root out' all those ideas that lurk in the hidden corners of your mind. They help you unblock those mental blocks!

Note Taking (taking notes from other people or books)

Suddenly it all becomes clear! Mind Maps help you see the appropriate links and connections as your teacher, book or computer reveals them. Everything makes more and more sense as time goes on.

Thinking

The Mind Map is the cool thinking tool, helping you to think: twice as well, twice as fast, twice as clearly and with much more fun.

Coming Up with Ideas

Now that you have seen how to Mind Map a short newspaper article, you can use the same method to turn whole **newspapers, books or folders full of notes** into **brain-friendly Mind Maps**. Later in this book, I will show you how to use Mind Maps to help you revise each of your different subjects at school.

What if you want to do more than simply remember things? What if you want to come up with some ideas of your own – a plan to write a story, for example, or a plan for a project.

Well, this is easy too. Your brain is the **most creative machine** on this planet! All you need is a Mind Map to set your endless store of ideas free.

'I CAN'T THINK OF ANYTHING TO WRITE!'

You have spent the weekend having a good time, seeing friends, playing games and computer games, mucking about and keeping something out of your mind. You have been using your fantastic brainpower to find excuses for ignoring it, while wishing you didn't have to do it. I think you know what I am talking about. Yes ... **the essay**!

Why is it that you are always given the world's worst titles when it comes to essays? We all know that if you were set to write an essay entitled 'Harry Potter and the Philosopher's Stone' life would be a whole lot easier. But no, instead, you are asked for three sides on 'The Lost Jug'.

Not a very inspiring title is it? It's the kind of title that is likely to lead to a Sunday night spent staring at a blank sheet of paper for a very long time, only to find you have 'lost' your homework when you are asked to hand it in the next day.

Why not put that blank sheet of paper to better use? **Why not try a Mind Map?** With a Mind Map and your amazing thinking ability you can make any story (including 'The Lost Jug'!) gripping.

1. Use a blank sheet of paper and some coloured pens.

2. In the centre of the page, draw a jug — a lost one!
   Colour it in and make it as elaborate as you want. This is a good way of getting your imagination working.

3. Draw your main branches coming away from the central picture.

4. Let your imagination run wild! Try to think of the most fantastical, magical, exciting things that could possibly be connected to this jug. Use the What–Where–When–Who–Why checkmap to help you. For example: When was it made? Where was it made? Who made it? What magical properties, if any, does it have? How old is it? Who owned or lost it? Why is it where it is?

5. Add this sub-topic information to your growing Mind Map, using symbols, codes, pictures and colours wherever you can.

6. Let your imagination continue to run riot. Use your next level of branches to add more exciting and intriguing details. The more you add, the more the whole story will become alive and clear in your mind (and in the mind of your reader).

7. Keep on going, adding branches further and further out, until you have enough information to write your masterpiece.

Look at the Mind Map on the next page and compare it with your own. Isn't it amazing how different our ideas are?

You see, you can be a good writer when yo

OWNER WILFRED WIZARD
25
TRENDY
SKATEBOARDER

STOLEN SUNDAY EVENING
"FINGERS" FRED TALL
THIN
35
LONDON
BURGLAR
SWAG

SHORT
FAT
55
BALD
DISHONEST

...se your brain the way it's designed to be used.

Chapter Three

Mind Maps® and School Stuff

Where your secret fo

This is where your **secret formula** will change your life for the better! In this chapter I will show you how you can apply your **new Mind Mapping skills** to your **school work**, helping you to ace those **exams**, wow your teachers and impress your friends into the bargain.

Mind Maps will help you **understand** things better, **remember** them well, **take notes more easily** and come up with lots of **brilliant ideas**. All this in every subject!

nula will change your life!

English

MIND YOUR PS AND QS

PPPP qqqq QQQQ qqqq pppp

There are many explanations as to the origin of this English phrase. Some include pleases and thank yous, some pints and quarts. All of them talk about choosing your language carefully, which is exactly what you need to do when writing an English essay.

Before you start to write, you need a **plan**, or in this case **a Mind Map**. Sometimes, planning might not feel like the best thing to do – especially when you are panicking about running out of time in an exam – but planning does save you time in the long run, and it can help you to produce an **A-grade story**, rather than a muddle of words and ideas. If you don't Mind Map and remain in panic-mode, you'll spend more time worrying than you will writing. You could end up with an essay that repeats itself and that is short and unbelievably dull.

Here is an example of a typical essay, taken from a European competition for 10–12 year olds who had to write an essay on 'My Summer Holidays'. As you read it, see if it is like any essays or thank-you letters you have written. With your new knowledge about Mind Mapping, decide where its weaknesses are and how you would improve it.

My Summer Holidays

This summer, our whole family went on our summer holiday. My father, Frederick, my mother, Jeanette, my big sister Lesley, my little brother, Gordon, and our two dogs, Rufus and Casper all came with me on our holidays this summer. We had a _Very_ good time. It was really fun. We went to see some great movies and had some great meals.

How bad is this essay? It repeats itself, it is badly organized and, most of all, dull.

Without Mind Maps essay writing can be really tough, producing low marks in return for lots of hard work and stress. With Mind Maps you will **save time, be more organized, come up with more ideas** for your essay, **have more fun** and **get better marks**.

What subject
are witches
best at?

Spelling!

MIND MAPPING ENGLISH

A Mind Map is the ideal of way of making sure you write a **brilliant essay** every time. It helps you put together all the **essential parts** of a perfect essay:

- *A **good introduction** that sets out what it is about*
- *Interesting and **imaginative content** – the main body of your story*
- *A **strong conclusion** that ties up all the loose ends and brings the tale to a satisfying end.*

Let's put these ideas put into practice as we use a Mind Map to plan a story called 'The Old Suitcase'.

THE OLD SUITCASE

One rainy day, when you are grown up, you decide to
explore the attic (garage, cellar, shed?) at your house.
You come across an old leather suitcase covered in dust
and cobwebs. You open the suitcase and find it full of
things that belonged to you when you were young. Each
object re-awakens a memory.

Choose any five things and describe the memories that
they produce, for example, an old pair of football boots,
damaged from when you had a tough match against your
arch-rivals, or an old photograph of all your school friends.

Remember, this story is set in the future, when you are
older and looking back on your youth, so some planning
is needed.

Mind Mapping The Old Suitcase

How might you Mind Map this story?

1. As always, begin with a central image that
   summarizes the topic to help to spark off ideas.
   In this case, a battered old suitcase would be a
   good image.

2. On one branch, plan your introduction. In this case you might
   want to set the scene, using main sub-topics to describe the day,
   the place and what happened.

3. Next, think about the body of your story. Here, you will describe the five items you came across in the suitcase and the memories they bring back. Put each one on a main sub-topic branch, ideally using pictures for each one (a picture is worth a thousand words!). Carry on adding second, third and fourth level detail branches as you let your imagination flow. This section of the Mind Map will probably be the most detailed as it is the main part of the story.

4. Finally, plan your conclusion. In this case, it could be your feelings about your finds. Try to find a final thought that summarizes your feelings about the day.

Once you have made a Mind Map, you will find that your essay will almost write itself. You have three clear sections mapped out – **an introduction, the content and a conclusion** – as well as plenty of colourful information with which to fill the story.

Using a Mind Map to plan an essay will make it so much easier to write. Have another good look at the sample Mind Map on page 40 before you start, then use it as a guide for your own, using pages 37 and 38. Start it off with a central image. Add branches from the centre as the ideas flow. Let your imagination help you write an **A-grade essay**.

Certificate

This is to certify that

[The Reader]

of this book is a genius of

Mind Mapping!

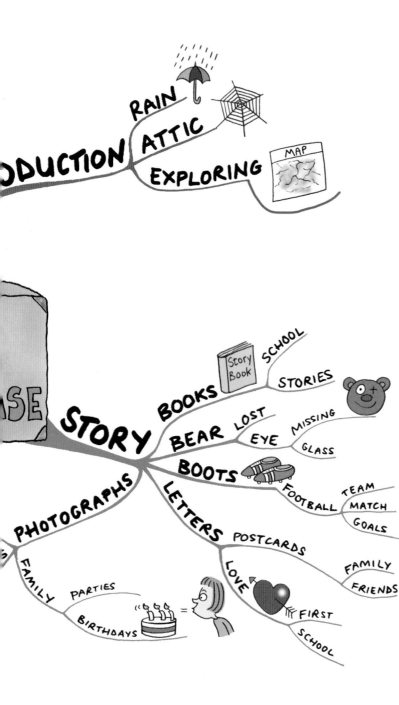

ODUCTION

RAIN

ATTIC

EXPLORING

MAP

ASE

STORY

BOOKS

Story Book

SCHOOL

STORIES

BEAR LOST

EYE

MISSING

GLASS

BOOTS

FOOTBALL

TEAM

MATCH

GOALS

LETTERS

POSTCARDS

FAMILY

FRIENDS

LOVE

FIRST

SCHOOL

PHOTOGRAPHS

FAMILY

PARTIES

BIRTHDAYS

A Family Outing

Imagine a family (give them a name) who are trying to decide where to go out to dinner. An argument follows, but eventually they decide on a restaurant. Write a story about what happens. You can use the pointers below to help you. I have highlighted the key words (main topics) to help you plan your Mind Map.

⭐ Set the **scene** – the time, place and the atmosphere.

⭐ Discussions on **place** – agreements and disagreements.

⭐ **Journey to the restaurant** – consider the route and any interesting sights or events on the way.

⭐ Describe the **outside and the inside of the restaurant** – perhaps model it on somewhere you have visited.

⭐ Choosing **what to eat** and **eating it** – use all your senses in describing the food!

⭐ Try to show the **characters** of the **individual members** of the family through what they say and do. Try to make the characters **original** and **memorable**.

⭐ Choose just one or two **incidents** during the meal and try to make them **interesting** and/or **amusing**. They should be things that could possibly happen in real life.

⭐ The **closing paragraph** is important. Make sure you round off your story with a **bang**!

Now give me a sentence with the word 'fascinate'.

My raincoat has ten buttons but I can only fasten eight.

BRAINTEASERS

1. There is one everyday English word that, when printed in capital letters, reads exactly the same upside down as it does the right way up. What is it?

2. These six words have something in common, what is it?
   Seperate
   Embarassed
   Adress
   Wierd
   Resteraunt
   Untill

Answers
1. NOON
2. They are all spelt incorrectly. The correct spellings are:
   Separate
   Embarrassed
   Address
   Weird
   Restaurant
   Until

History

MAGICAL HISTORY TOUR

Wouldn't it be fun if you really could magic yourself to another time? You could be cheering on your favourite gladiator or braving the waves in a Viking boat. Whatever your dream tour of past times is, learning history should be *fun*, not just a mind-boggling collection of names and dates to remember.

On the pages that follow are some fascinating historical stories on which you can try out your **new Mind Mapping skills**. I'll give you guidelines along the way ...

What subject
are snakes
best at?

Hiss-tory!

MIND MAPPING HISTORY

800 AD - A Viking Invasion

The Vikings were feared throughout Europe, but some might say that a history test is more frightening. If you **use a Mind Map** to help you with your **note-taking** and **revision**, you will have nothing to fear!

The Mind Map on page 46 summarizes all the information in the article opposite in a way that is really easy to remember. Again, there is a central image that sums up the main subject. Here a longboat has been drawn to represent the Viking invasion. The **main sub-topics** of the article are on the branches coming away from the central image. **Sub-topics** and **details** are written on further branches.

A VIKING INVASION

In about 800 AD the Vikings began their infamous raids, spreading terror!

Most raids were carried out by small parties of up to 10 boats, each with 30 warriors on board.

The speed of their boats meant they could make surprise attacks and then get away fast. The Vikings were known to be brave but brutal warriors. Wherever they went, they spread terror and panic.

One of the reasons people were so scared of the Vikings was because they had some of the best armour and weapons in Europe. They fought mainly with swords, spears, bows and axes. The ordinary warriors wore tough leather tunics, while the wealthier ones wore armour made from chainmail. As well as this, all Vikings carried a large round shield, which was sometimes covered with leather.

The most feared Viking warriors were the berserkers. To make them fiercer, these warriors may have been drugged so they would lose control of themselves. The word 'berserk' is still used today to describe someone who has lost control.

At first, the Vikings raided rich churches for loot. Later, they started attacking towns, looting and plundering, then burning most of them to the ground. They showed no mercy to the terrified women or children and a lot were murdered. Many women were tortured before they died. Some were taken prisoner and used or sold as slaves.

By Orderic Vitalis
Warfare Chronicler
© Daily Mail

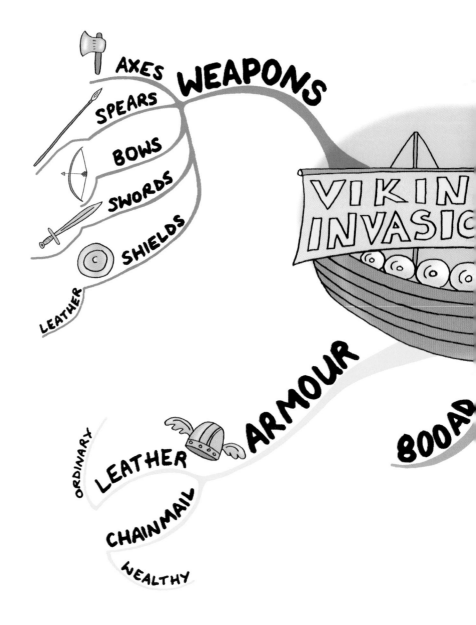

WEAPONS

AXES

SPEARS

BOWS

SWORDS

SHIELDS

LEATHER

VIKIN
INVASIO

ARMOUR

LEATHER

ORDINARY

CHAINMAIL

WEALTHY

800AD

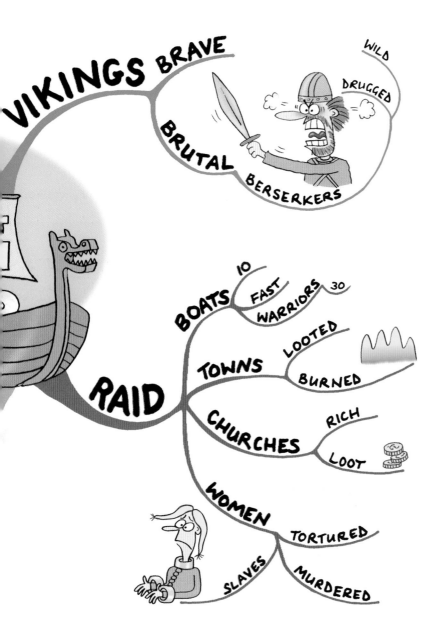

VIKINGS BRAVE

WILD

DRUGGED

BRUTAL BERSERKERS

RAID

BOATS 10 FAST

WARRIORS 30

TOWNS LOOTED

BURNED

CHURCHES RICH

LOOT

WOMEN TORTURED

SLAVES MURDERED

The Romans were at it too. In around 150 AD they ruled an empire that covered most of what we now know as Europe, and beyond, to Palestine, Egypt and North Africa. They did it with a giant army who fought some of the greatest battles of all time.

A Mind Map on a subject like 'The Roman Army' could tell you a lot about the history, geography and the ordinary people of Rome at the time. The **checkmap** opposite would work well here. Read the article on page 50 and try to put a **one-word answer to each question** on the big branches, and add smaller branches for your own explanations.

Father:
I see from your report that you're doing badly in history.

Son:
I can't help it. He keeps asking me about things that happened before I was born.

ROMAN SOLDIERS

They were grouped into large numbers called legions, made up of 5,000 soldiers.

Each legion was made up of 5,000 heavily armed foot soldiers and some cavalry.

The legion included engineers, surveyors, stonemasons and carpenters, as well as other craftsmen.

As well as fighting major battles, the legions built forts, bridges and roads. Only citizens of the Empire could join the legions. They joined for 25 years. When they retired they were given money (three gold coins) and land to farm.

Most of the actual fighting was done by soldiers called auxiliaries. They were not citizens of the Empire. They were made citizens when they retired. They included cavalry from Spain and Hungary and archers from the Middle East. After about AD 100, the Empire stopped growing. The army then spent most of its time keeping hold on the lands that it had captured. This took a lot of men. More and more non-citizens were recruited as auxiliaries to defend the forts on the borders of the Empire.

Tribes people, from outside the Empire, were also employed. They were put in regiments called numeri. Like the auxiliaries, the numeri often defended the forts on the frontiers. They were not made citizens when they retired.

By Orderic Vitalis
Warfare Chronicler
© *Daily Mail*

BRAINTEASERS

1. Why would the Romans have called Britain's first full-length motorway 1001?

2. Admiral Lord Nelson is standing on top of his column in the middle of Trafalgar Square facing west. Given the instructions:

   ★ Right turn! (90 degrees)
   ★ About turn! (180 degrees)
   ★ Left turn (90 degrees)

   which way would he end up facing?

Answers

1. Because 1001 is MI in Roman numerals.

2. East

Mathematics

Did you think that mathematics couldn't be put onto a Mind Map?

Mind Maps are marvellous for maths because mathematics is not, as many students think, millions of formulas and equations. All those formulas and equations are based on the most important part of mathematics – a few basic underlying concepts and ideas. It is these that are most important, and these that a Mind Map helps you to sort out in your brain.

Did you hear about the schoolboy who couldn't get to grips with decimals?

He just couldn't see the point.

The Mind Map will give you a **clearer idea** of what branch of mathematics you are studying, will help you **clarify those areas** you need help with from your teacher, and will help you **understand where the formulas and equations actually do fit in**. The Mind Map will also show you the areas where your maths brain is already brilliant – and these will increasingly be more than you thought. The Mind Map helps you **get your maths brain in gear**.

Remember: The number of branches you add is totally up to you.

Make sure you know the difference between a triangle and a triceratops! In this Mind Map, Mr Big, the triceratops, will teach you all about triangles.

What's the best way to pass a geometry test?

Know all the angles.

3 EQUAL ANGLES

EQUILATERAL

SIDES

3 EQUAL

TRIA

1 90° ANGLES

RIGHT-ANGLED

ANY LENGTH SIDES

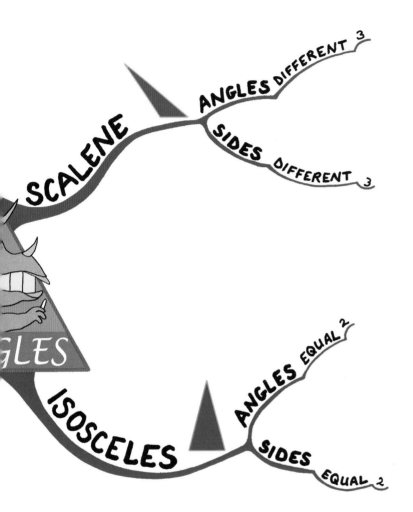

SCALENE
ANGLES DIFFERENT 3
SIDES DIFFERENT 3

GLES

ISOSCELES
ANGLES EQUAL 2
SIDES EQUAL 2

Now look at the information that follows on quadrilaterals. Use the material to produce your own Mind Map on quadrilaterals, just like Mr Big's triangle Mind Map. Add as many branches as you need.

Quadrilaterals have four sides

SQUARE

4 sides of equal length, and 4 right angles.

This symbol tells you it's a right angle.

RECTANGLE

2 pairs of equal sides, and 4 right angles.

RHOMBUS

A square pushed over: 4 sides of equal length, opposite sides are parallel, and opposite angles are equal.

PARALLELOGRAM

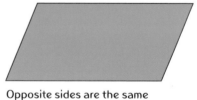

Opposite sides are the same length and parallel.

TRAPEZIUM

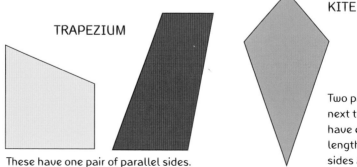

These have one pair of parallel sides.

KITE

Two pairs of sides next to each other have equal lengths, but no sides are parallel.

1. How many triangles can you find in this diagram?

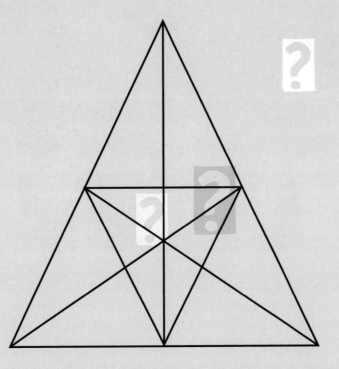

2. Find a number whose double exceeds its half by 99.

Mind Maps and School Stuff

Answers
1. At least 47.
2. 66

Science

THERE'S SOMETHING FISHY IN THE AIR

Is it lunch? No! It's coming from the science lab where somebody is experimenting with gases!

You will be doing all kinds of experimenting when you look at materials in science. All materials are the same in that they are all made up of tiny particles. At the same time they vary a lot. Do you find this confusing? All will be made clear and simple by Mind Maps that help you remember where the differences and similarities lie.

Why is school like a shower?

One wrong turn and you are in hot water!

You can use a Mind Map to discover the properties of solids, liquids and gases and master those molecules!

I started off this Mind Map with the **three main groups** into which materials can be put. I then used the **main branches** to define the **properties** of each group, and the **smaller branches** for **examples**.

Solids

Example: cheese

⭐ *All the particles in solids are packed tightly together and can hardly move.*
⭐ *Solids keep their shape.*
⭐ *Solids can be cut or shaped.*
⭐ *Anything you can grab hold of is solid.*
⭐ *Solids are easy to control.*

Liquids

Example: water

⭐ *The particles in liquids are not so tightly packed and can move a little.*
⭐ *Liquids are runny and flow downwards with gravity.*
⭐ *Liquids take up the shape of any container into which they are poured.*
⭐ *The surface of a liquid in a container stays level.*
⭐ *Liquids are more difficult to control.*

Gases

Example: gas fire

⭐ *The particles in gases have lots of room and move around all the time.*
⭐ *Gases are always spreading into an empty space around us.*
⭐ *Most gases are invisible.*

Mind Maps and School Stuff

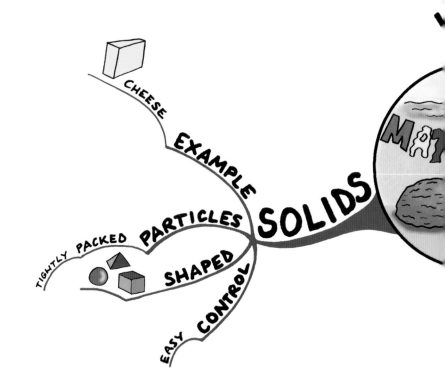

CHEESE

EXAMPLE

SOLIDS

TIGHTLY PACKED PARTICLES

SHAPED

EASY CONTROL

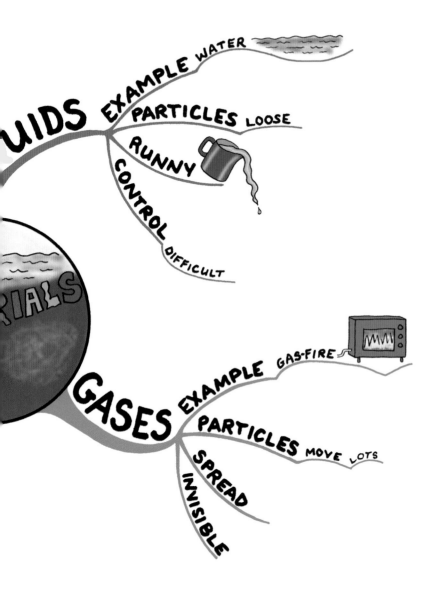

UIDS EXAMPLE WATER

PARTICLES LOOSE

RUNNY

CONTROL DIFFICULT

RIALS

GASES EXAMPLE GAS-FIRE

PARTICLES MOVE LOTS

SPREAD

INVISIBLE

Read the information below about reversible and irreversible changes then transfer the information onto your Mind Map. Remember to look for **key words** (some have been highlighted in colour to help you), and ask yourself what the main reason is that a change is not reversible. What has happened to the material? The central image on the Mind Map has been filled in to help you get started.

CHANGING MATERIALS

Look at the two experiments below. Making a candle is an example of a reversible change. Burning a candle is an example of an irreversible change.

Experiment 1 – Making a Candle

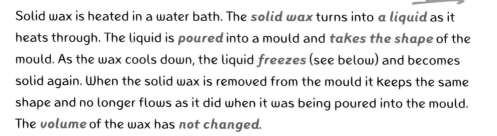

Solid wax is heated in a water bath. The *solid wax* turns into *a liquid* as it heats through. The liquid is *poured* into a mould and *takes the shape* of the mould. As the wax cools down, the liquid *freezes* (see below) and becomes solid again. When the solid wax is removed from the mould it keeps the same shape and no longer flows as it did when it was being poured into the mould. The *volume* of the wax has *not changed*.

This is a *reversible change* because the solid wax changed to a liquid, then back to a solid again without any being lost or added, so there was no change in the material's properties.

Did you know?:
'Freezing' is the scientific term for the process of a liquid turning into a solid as it cools down.

Experiment 2 – Burning a Candle

The wick of a candle is lit. The wax *burns*, giving off light, heat and smoke. If the candle is left to burn it becomes *smaller*. In other words, the volume of the wax has *changed*.

This is an *irreversible change* because something has been lost from the candle.

What's the most important thing to remember in chemistry?

Never lick the spoon!

BRAINTEASER

Which is heavier: a kilo of feathers or a kilo of iron?

They both weigh the same – one kilo.

Answer

Geography

Without actually visiting every country in the world, it is difficult to imagine what each country is like, and how landscapes, coastlines and the weather can be so different from those we know in our own country.

It is important that we are aware of the *geography* of our world though, so take a few imaginative steps into your brain and start planning a round-the-world trip!

MIND MAPPING GEOGRAPHY

It is possible to get round the world in 20 minutes, if you use a Mind Map! And there is no chance of you getting lost!

Did you hear about the brilliant geography teacher?

He had abroad knowledge of his subject!

UK
Cool Temperate Maritime.
Our winters aren't that cold,
but our summers aren't too
hot either! And never go out
without an umbrella.

CANADA
Cool Temperate.
Rainfall throughout
the year, with warmer
summers and colder
winters (often below
freezing).

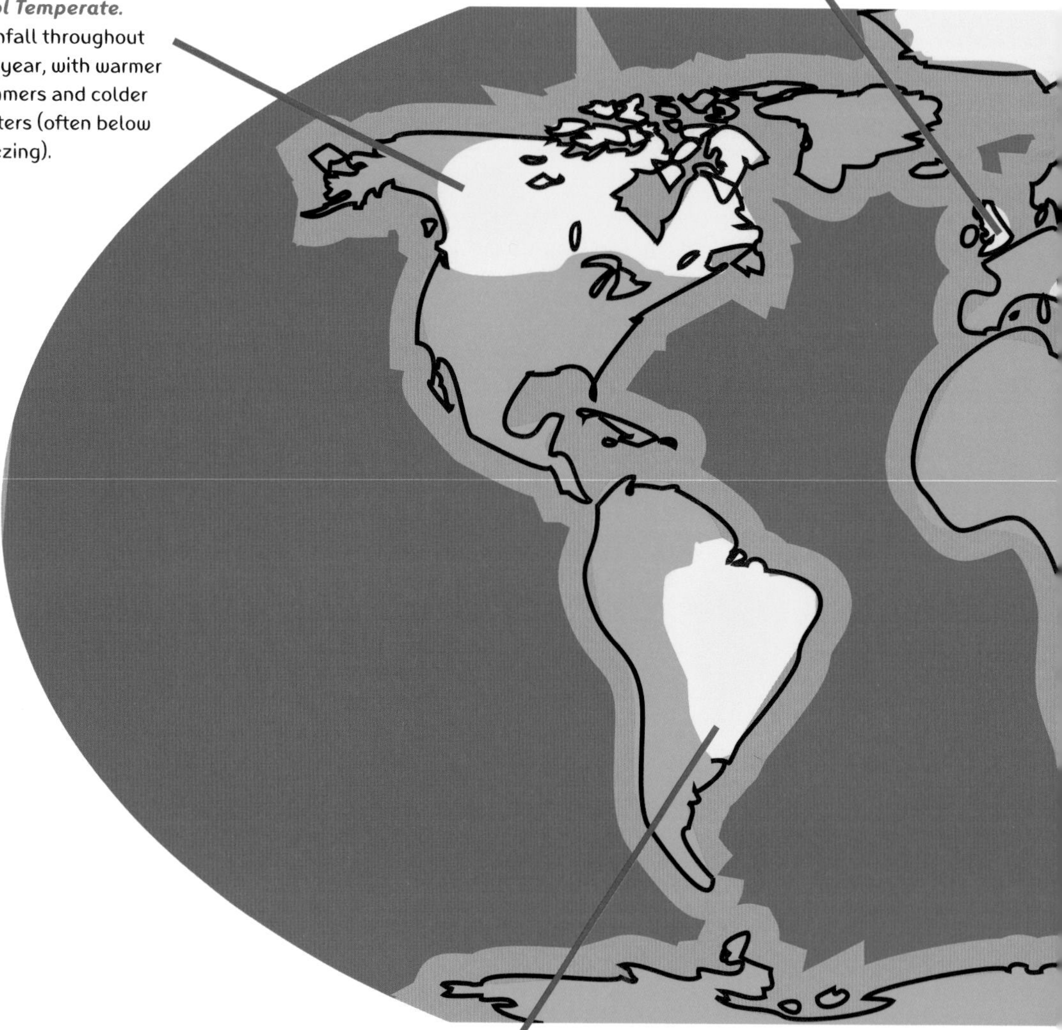

BRAZIL
Equatorial Wet.
It's just as hot as Egypt,
but rainy too.

POLE
Polar.
Very cold all year round.
The sun shines, but you
won't be taking your
clothes off to sunbathe!

ITALY
Mediterranean.
You will be much more aware
of the four seasons here, with
hot and dry summers, going
into cooler, wetter winters.

EGYPT
Tropical Dry.
It is hot and dry all year
here, just as deserts
should be! Remember,
though, that deserts get
very cold at night.

0   2000 miles

2000 km

INDIA
Tropical Wet/Dry.
In these areas it will be hot
all year with the possibility
of one or two rainy seasons.
Sudden, very heavy rainfall
is usual, known as a monsoon.

Did you know ... In India, the
monsoons from June to
September provide almost 90%
of the country's water supply.

Mind Maps and School Stuff

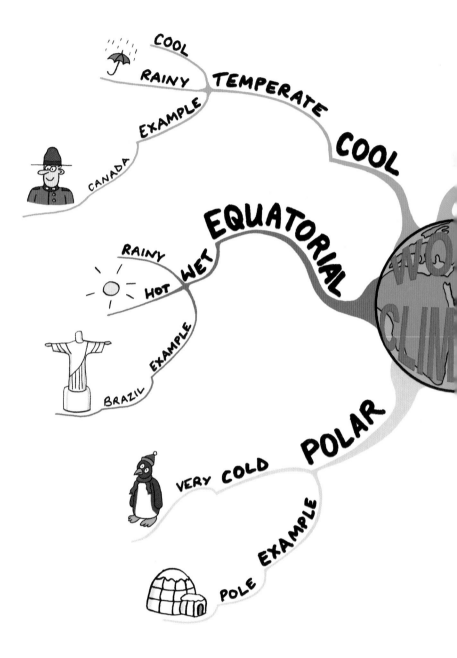

COOL

RAINY

TEMPERATE

COOL

EXAMPLE

CANADA

EQUATORIAL

RAINY

HOT

WET

EXAMPLE

BRAZIL

POLAR

VERY COLD

POLE EXAMPLE

WORLD CLIMATE

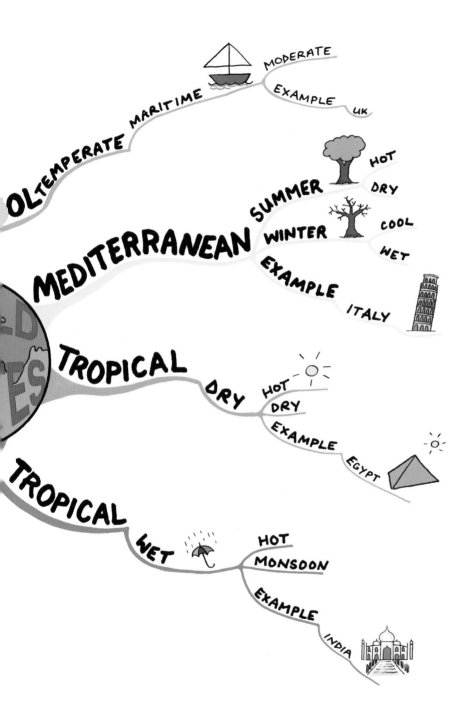

OL TEMPERATE MARITIME — MODERATE

EXAMPLE — UK

MEDITERRANEAN
SUMMER — HOT / DRY
WINTER — COOL / WET
EXAMPLE — ITALY

TROPICAL DRY — HOT / DRY
EXAMPLE — EGYPT

TROPICAL WET — HOT / MONSOON
EXAMPLE — INDIA

Teacher:
What is the
climate of New
Zealand?

Girl:
Very cold,
Sir!

Teacher:
Wrong.

Girl:
But, Sir! When we
buy New Zealand
lamb, it is always
frozen.

OVER TO YOU!

Water, water everywhere! It's true, water is all around us, but not always in obvious places, like in the air we breathe. Let's get one thing straight: the water cycle does not have two wheels and a bell. It is the process of evaporation and condensation of water in the air, which is going on around us all the time, so you should know about it.

Read the notes opposite about the water cycle and see if you can turn them into a Mind Map. Remember that **evaporation** and **condensation** are the **two key processes**, so use them as a starting point.

Organizing
Ever feel overwhelmed by all the masses of information coming in at you? Mind Maps help put it all together.

The Water Cycle

Evaporation and condensation of water in the air. It keeps going all the time.

Evaporation - turning into a gas

1) The sun can heat water. The water goes into the air – it doesn't disappear. The water evaporates into a gas.

A LIQUID EVAPORATES INTO A GAS WHEN IT IS WARMED

puddle

2) The water from wet clothes evaporates into the air.

Condensation - turning a gas back into a liquid

1) Water vapour in the air cools and turns into water droplets.
2) The water vapour condenses.

A GAS CONDENSES INTO A LIQUID WHEN IT IS COOLED

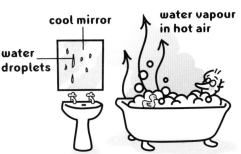

cool mirror

water droplets

water vapour in hot air

Evaporation and Condensation of Water on Planet Earth

1) The water here on planet Earth is constantly recycling. Strange but true.
2) When the temperature gets really low rain drops can fall as snow or hail instead of rain.

WATER CYCLE – SOUNDS LIKE A CROSS-CHANNEL BIKE ...
Remember that ice, water and steam are all states of water. You really do need to know the words evaporation and condensation. Don't forget that water doesn't disappear when it evaporates, but it turns into a gas. Look carefully at the diagram of the water cycle below, and try to follow the water on its way around the picture.

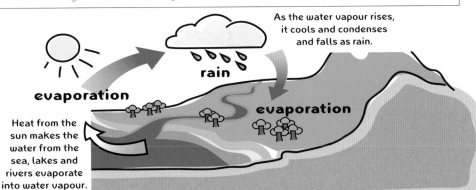

As the water vapour rises, it cools and condenses and falls as rain.

rain

evaporation

evaporation

Heat from the sun makes the water from the sea, lakes and rivers evaporate into water vapour.

71

BRAINTEASERS

1. What has cities without houses, woods without trees and rivers with no water?

2. With nothing to hand except a three-litre jug and a five-litre jug, how can you measure out exactly one litre of water?

Mind Maps for Kids

Do you doodle? Did you know that most people doodle? They do! Doodling is not a waste of time and it helps you to not lose concentration.

Lots of recent studies show that doodling helps your concentration and is a great memory booster. A Mind Map is the most sophisticated doodle imaginable!

Do doodle, do!

Modern Foreign Languages

PAWS FOR THOUGHT

Teacher:
Are you good at
French?

Boy:
Well, yes
and no.

Teacher:
What do you
mean, yes
and no?

Boy:
Yes, I am no
good at
French!

Many people think that learning a modern foreign language can be difficult. It can, if you don't Mind Map. Like English and mathematics, modern foreign languages are simply a matter of understanding a few basic concepts and ideas. Mind Maps, once again, are the way ...

MIND MAPPING A FOREIGN LANGUAGE

Mind Maps are a great way of remembering. You can use them to help you **recall vocabulary** and **grammar**. The drawing on page 76 shows how Mind Maps can help you remember those tricky verbs.

Paws, the cat opposite, is here to show you that some things about a language are simply a question of learning the rules. (His whiskers seem to make a rather good starter for a Mind Map.) He chose to put his French hat on for this example.

This is grammar the French Way (which rhymes with 'beret', which is what Paws has on his head). In French, there are three different kinds of verbs: those that end in **-er**, those that end in **-ir** and those that end in **-re**. Each type of verb follows a set pattern or 'conjugation'.

ER VERBS

infinitive   **present**
jouer (to play)   je joue
                  tu joues
                  il joue/elle joue

imperative
joue
joue!   nous jouons
jouons!   vous jouez
jouez!   ils jouent/elles jouent

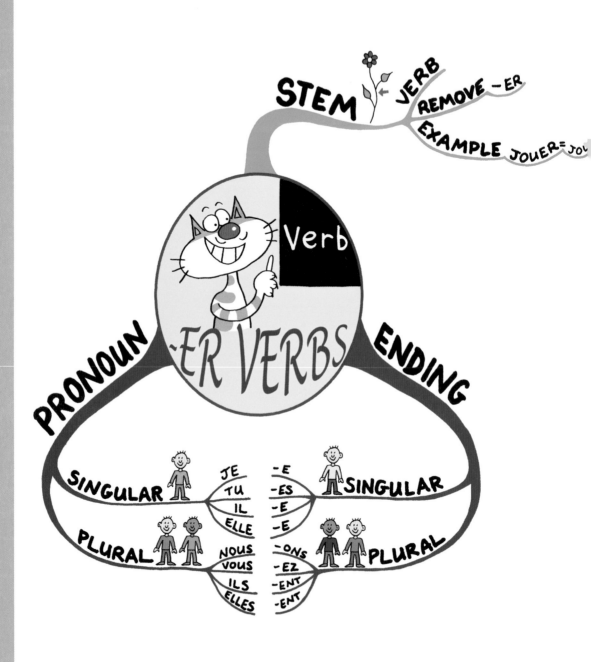

STEM

VERB

REMOVE −ER

EXAMPLE JOUER = JOU

Verb

-ER VERBS

PRONOUN

ENDING

SINGULAR

JE
TU
IL
ELLE

−E
−ES
−E
−E

SINGULAR

PLURAL

NOUS
VOUS
ILS
ELLES

−ONS
−EZ
−ENT
−ENT

PLURAL

ER ... what was that?

That was **-er** verbs. There are also **-ir** and **-re** verbs. Can you use the cat's whiskers to sort those out too?

IR VERBS

infinitive	present
choisir (to choose)	je choisis
	tu choisis
imperative	il choisit/elle choisit/on choisit
choisis!	nous choisissons
choisissons!	vous choisissez
choisissez!	ils choisissent/elles choisissent

What did you
learn at school
today?

Not enough, I
have to go back
tomorrow

RE VERBS

infinitive	present
vendre (to sell)	je vend**s**
	tu vend**s**
imperative	il vend/elle vend/on vend
vends!	nous vend**ons**
vendons!	vous vend**ez**
vendez!	ils vend**ent**/elles vend**ent**

Teacher:
Where is the
English
Channel?

Boy:
I don't know,
our TV doesn't
pick it up.

BRAINTEASERS

1. Two Germans are going for a swim. One German is the father of the other German's son. How are the two Germans related?

2. Which word do English speakers from France always pronounce wrongly?

Answers

1. They are husband and wife.
2. Wrongly.

Chapter Four

How to Ace Exams

With Mind Maps®, you can eat books for breakfast! You can condense a ☆ book and any chapter of a book onto a single page, **and** you can remember the lot!

Ace Exams with

The Game of Examinations

Have you ever wondered how some kids seem to **ace exams** while others struggle, even sometimes when you know that those who get Cs know more than those who got the As?

It's probably because the A student knows the **rules of the game**, but the C student doesn't.

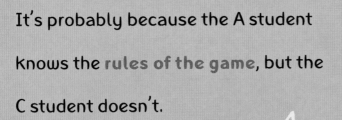

The Mind Map is not only the **secret formula** that helps you 'A'ce those exams. The Mind Map holds all the **secret clues** to the game and helps you come out winning! Once again it's a case of 'same brain/different method'. The Mind Map leads you to success.

a simple Mind Map

Cramming

'Cramming doesn't work, right?'

'Right!'

'And wrong!'

'How can it be both right and wrong?'

'Easy! It depends how you do it.'

'Most students cram (desperately!) at the end of the year, just before exams.'

The reason why this usually does not work is because it is the same as stuffing your body full of food just before a sports competition. You know what happens when you exercise on a much-too-full stomach.

If you cram just before the exam, you stuff your brain to the point where it gives you mental blocks in the exam. The information disappears almost immediately after the exam anyway and so the whole exercise is a fear-producing, sick-making waste of time.

Mind Maps for Kids

Cramming can work if you use Mind Maps to help you cram *at the beginning of the year!* For each topic that you study you create a Mind Map, which will help you absorb the **ideas** and **facts** that come to you. It will also serve as a **handy revision sheet** for when it comes to the exam.

Quickly scan the relevant sections of your textbook, as if you were flipping through the book in a bookshop. Ideally, with the help of a friend or two, you could **discuss the main ideas of the topic**, and Mind Map the basic idea-skeleton of the topic and all its main and second level ideas.

The advantage of this is huge. What you have done with your Master Mind Map is to lay a **giant** net that will naturally catch the '**butterflies**' of all new ideas that come to you, *without any extra effort on your behalf*. These ideas might appear in lectures from your teachers, books, your computer screen, ideas from friends, and your own ideas and original thoughts.

Every time a **new idea** (butterfly) floats into view, your automatic Mind Map Supernet will 'net it'.

Every time you catch a butterfly-idea, the butterfly adds itself to the net and becomes *part of the net*. So every time you catch a new idea, your net gets even bigger and more capable of catching more new ideas. So the school year rolls on, with everything getting easier and easier and easier.

In addition, each one of those new ideas will automatically be reviewing everything you already know. So **revision** becomes a **natural process** rather than some massive added load you have to bury yourself under at the end of the school year.

Preparing for exams and reviewing
Mind Maps help you review everything at once because all the information is on one page, which your brain can 'photograph'.

The Exam Itself

'Exams are pretty tough and scary, right?'

'Wrong! With Mind Maps, they can be a breeze.'

'Because you are always under time pressure in exams, it is best to read the question and get straight into the answer, right?'

'Wrong! You can play it cool by using a Mind Map.'

Look at the question and then Mind Map for up to 10 minutes. This gets your brain **in gear, fishes out all the necessary and important information** for answering the question, and at the same time **organizes it** so that it is immediately ready for writing down.

You use your Mind Map in an exam in exactly the same way you do for writing an essay (look back at page 27 if you need to refresh your memory). Put the **main point** of your answer in the **centre**, your **main sub-topics** on the main branches, and decreasing level of details on the outer limits of your Mind Map.

You can then sit back and let your Mind Map, pen and hand race to the finish line ahead of everyone else!

Writing exams
If you use Mind Maps, you will find you can write two- to ten-times more in exams, and everything you write will be of a higher quality.

Chapter Five

Fun Stuff

Mind Maps are

The sky's the limit! There is **no end** to what you can Mind Map®. It doesn't all have to be about schoolwork. Mind Maps are an ideal way of getting your life sorted.

Mind Maps help you to plan things out and they help you come up with awesome ideas. If you want to hold the greatest party, live in the best bedroom and come up with a wicked web page, a Mind Map could be the **secret of your success.**

or fun stuff too!

Party Planning – Mind Mapping It Large!

When you have an **exciting event** coming up, like a party, it can be really useful to **think ahead**. A little planning goes a long way towards making things run more smoothly and successfully. You and everyone can then enjoy it without worrying about what has been forgotten ...

Planning
In the same way that football teams, armies and explorers plan ahead by seeing the whole picture with all the good and bad possibilities, Mind Maps help you plan the events, competitions and adventures of your life.

Will you have a birthday any time soon? If not, I'm sure you can think of a good enough reason to have a party or get-together with your mates. What would your ideal party be?

The Mind Map on page 90 is a blueprint for a birthday party, but maybe you have party ambitions that go beyond a barbecue at your house. Perhaps you have a better option, such as going to a football match? Or perhaps a cinema screening, just for you and your mates? Or a disco?

With your imagination working overtime, th

Using the Mind Mind provided as an example, try to map out your own perfect party.

★ *Draw a picture in the middle of the page to represent your party.*
★ *You could draw a birthday cake, or a balloon.*
★ *Next draw your big, main branches coming off this picture. They will represent the main things you need to think about when planning your party. Remember to do each branch in a different colour to make it stand out. You might want to use the following list to help you:*

- Why are you having the party?
- When will it be?
- Where will you hold it?
- Who will you invite?
- What activities will you include?
- Are you going to have a theme?
- Will you serve food and, if so, what will you have?
- Will there be any music?

These questions are just to get you started; there may be other things that are important to your perfect party.

★ *Once you have decided what you need to think about and have drawn in the main branches, you can really get down to making plans. Draw further branches off the main ones, so you can put in all the details. If, say, you are thinking of having music, what kind of music will there be? Will there be a DJ, will you just play CDs or will you all gather round the piano and sing?! Draw a different branch for each of your options.*
★ *You can carry on adding extra branches and putting in as much detail as you like. It's amazing how many ideas you can come up with as all the things you might not have thought of if you hadn't used a Mind Map keep on popping into your head.*

arty will certainly be a party to remember!

Fun Stuff

FANCY

CASUAL

DRESS

THEME

KETCHUP

BURGERS

RIBS

BARBECUE

HOT DOGS

ICE CREAM

FOOD

PAR

CAKE

BIRTHDAY

SNACKS

CRISPS

CDs

MUSIC

HIRE

SOUND SYSTEM

OWN

TAPES

D.J.

MIX

HIRE

PRE-RECORD

FRIEND

Mind Maps for Kids

WHEN?

DATE — APRIL 2nd — SATURDAY — BIRTHDAY

TIME — DAY — EVENING

WHERE?

HOME

HIRE — HALL — VILLAGE

POOL — SWIMMING

CENTRE — COMMUNITY

WHO?

FRIENDS — SCHOOL × 10

FAMILY — MUM — DAD — BROTHER — GRAN

Sort That Bedroom!

Be honest – how long has it been since you actually tidied your bedroom? If you did tidy it, how much stuff have you shoved under your bed? Is your bed actually floating off the floor on a platform of papers, old toys, magazines, clothes, etc., etc.?

Sorting your room can be a painful process, but if you are really being nagged to get things in order you can use a Mind Map to **make the job speedier and easier and to get in your parents' good books**! In addition, you can use that same Mind Map to help you design the bedroom you have always wanted.

After all, do you actually need that Teletubbies book that has been gathering dust under your bed? Do you want people to think you still read it? Best get to work. Who knows what other horrors are lurking under there!

MIND MAPPING
A VA-VA-VROOM BEDROOM

Page 94 shows how you can use a Mind Map to get the bedroom you **really want** – and one that has **ooomph**! It's not just about getting rid of all your junk. You can also Mind Map exactly how you want your bedroom to **look** and **feel**. You can use the Mind Map to plan how to arrange your furniture, your posters and your bits and pieces.

★ To begin, draw a little **picture** in the middle of the page that sums up your bedroom.

★ Next, imagine what your **ideal bedroom** is going to be like. What colours? What posters? What main objects? What sounds? What general 'feel'? From these imaginings select your main branches and connect them, in different colours, to your central picture. All your second level and detail ideas flow out from these main branches. Use images and colours wherever you can.

★ Include everything you want to chuck out, everything you want to keep and reorder, and special new things you need to make your bedroom ideal.

★ Keep going until you have a foolproof plan for the perfect bedroom. The only thing you need to do now is put the plan into action.

When you have completed your Mind Map and transformed your bedroom, send me a copy of the Mind Map and a picture of your va-va-vroom bedroom. I look forward to seeing them. For details of where to send your completed Mind Maps, turn to page 117.

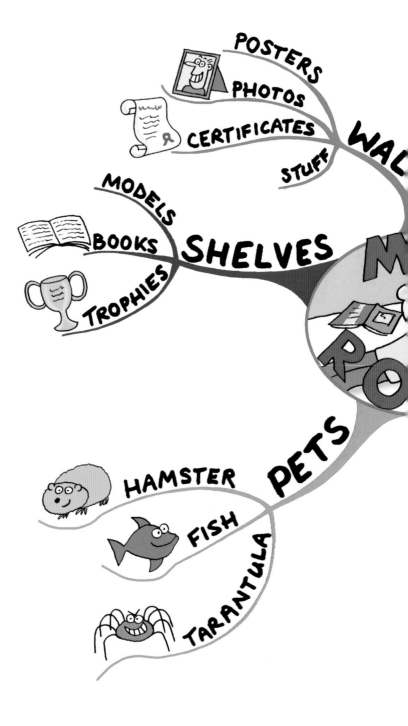

POSTERS

PHOTOS

CERTIFICATES

STUFF

WAL

MODELS

BOOKS

SHELVES

TROPHIES

M

R O

HAMSTER

FISH

PETS

TARANTULA

CHANGE

WHY? TIP! BORING

WHEN? NOW URGENT

HOW? FURNITURE MOVE

COLOUR WALLS
CARPET

PLAN ROOM
WINDOWS
DOORS
SOCKETS
LIGHTS

CLUTTER KEEP

CHUCK

CHARITY SHOP

SWAP

Planning a Project

There is nothing like the school holidays, stretching endlessly in front of you with nothing for you to do but put your feet up, enjoy your hobbies, catch up on some quality television and hang out with your mates. Unless, of course, you are set *a project!*

Countless perfectly good school holidays have been ruined by nasty projects set on the last day of term, but you really don't have to let school projects ruin your holidays. A Mind Map can make the job **easy**, **quick** and, believe it or not, *fun!*

On page 97 there is a Mind Map plan for organising a school open day. The Mind Map plans out the project in six easy steps – or branches.

On pages 98-9 is a Mind Map template for mapping out your thoughts for *any project*. As usual, always start with a **central image**, using **six main branches**, one for each the steps you need to follow. I have made the key words bold to help you choose images for your main branches.

1. What is the project for? It might be, as in this case, for a school open day, or perhaps it is part of your coursework.

2. What is your target? It is always good to have a target at which to aim. In the example on page 98, the project is part of a competition and the aim is to win. Your aim might be to get top marks – or just to finish the project in time.

3. What is the theme? This is very important and can lead to several branches of Mind Map thoughts as more ideas occur to you.

4. What are you going to do/make? What suits your project best? Are you going to write it up, make a model, a scrapbook, a picture?

5. How will you research it? What resources do you have? The range is great – you could use the Internet, the library or interview people.

6. Finally, the timing! When will you start it? When will you finish it? Break down each of the stages into an achievable timetable to make it seem more manageable.

Your Project Mind Map will make the project **more creative, more organized, more easy to keep control of** and will **save you loads of time**. It also makes it much more easy to involve your family and friends, who will help to make the task less of a bore and more of a game. Not to mention the **good grades** you will get!

Overviewing
Mind Maps help you to see the 'whole picture'. They put everything in context and give you power over your subject.

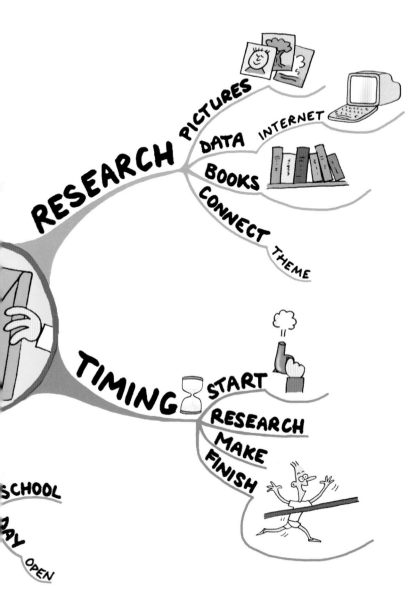

RESEARCH

PICTURES

DATA — INTERNET

BOOKS

CONNECT — THEME

TIMING — START

RESEARCH

MAKE

FINISH

SCHOOL

AY — OPEN

Your Dream Shop

Do you ever get dragged round the shops with your Mum? How boring is it?
Very! These shopping trips usually take place just before the beginning of the
school year, when you have grown out of your school uniform, or when you
have worn down your shoes to nothing. There is nothing worse than shopping
for school stuff. The shops that sell school stuff are so dull. Usually they
contain just racks of uniforms or sensible shoes – and not a Game Cube or an X
Box in sight!

If you had your own shop, things would be different. Shopping would be awesome. Imagine a shop where everything was *free* and where you could get *absolutely anything* you wanted. What things would you have on offer?

The Mind Map on page 102 is a sample of one boy's dream shop. As you can see, **the possibilities are endless!** The shop has things to eat, things to do, things to watch, things to read, things to wear. You name it, this shop's got it!

 *Map out your own dream shop on a sheet of paper. Start with a **central image** that sums up your shop. It might be a picture of the shop itself, as in this case, or maybe you could sketch in a great big shopping bag.*

 *Draw in some **thick coloured lines** to represent all the types of things you would like to stock in your shop. These might include sweets, clothes, books, sports equipment or computer games.*

⭐ *Write in the names and draw a little picture, if you like. Once you have done this, draw some thinner lines coming off each item and write in more details. Keep on adding more **detail**. Remember, in this shop, everything is free, so you can really go wild. And once you have finished your Mind Map, perhaps you can drag your Mum round your own shop!*

Fun Stuff

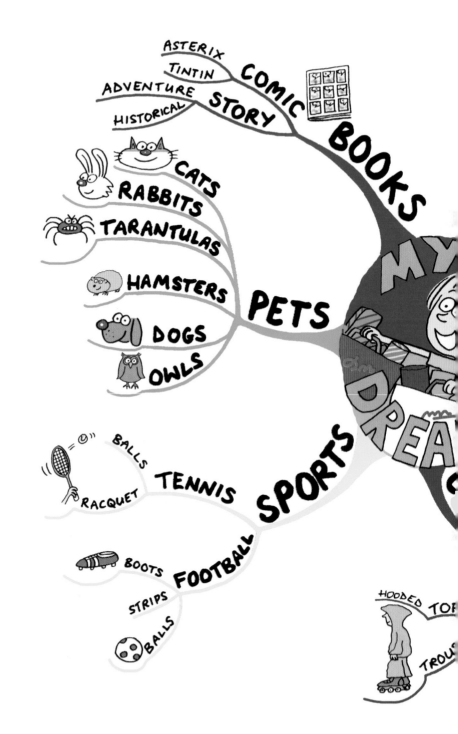

ASTERIX
TINTIN
ADVENTURE
HISTORICAL
COMIC
STORY
BOOKS

CATS
RABBITS
TARANTULAS
HAMSTERS
DOGS
OWLS
PETS

MY
DREA

BALLS
RACQUET
TENNIS
SPORTS

BOOTS
STRIPS
BALLS
FOOTBALL

HOODED TOP
TROUS

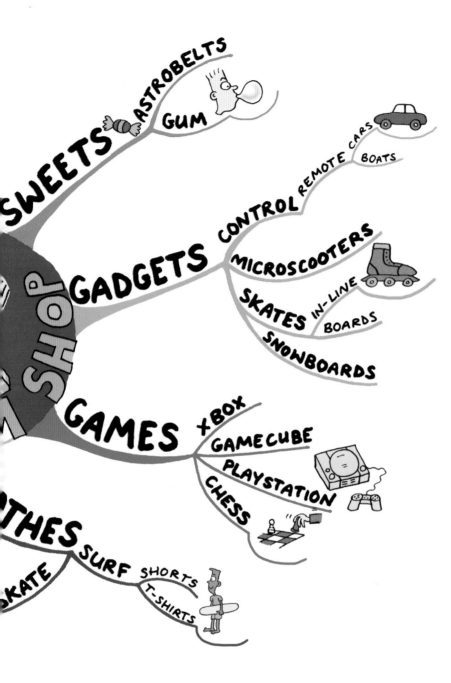

SWEETS
ASTROBELTS
GUM

GADGETS
CONTROL
REMOTE
CARS
BOATS
MICROSCOOTERS
SKATES
IN-LINE
BOARDS
SNOWBOARDS

SHOP

GAMES
XBOX
GAMECUBE
PLAYSTATION
CHESS

THES
SKATE
SURF
SHORTS
T-SHIRTS

Do the Write Thing!

Getting a letter through the post is cool! You might be on email, but there is still nothing better than ripping open that envelope when it comes through the door. 'As long as it's not my school report!' I hear you say. If you have been Mind Mapping and getting those better marks, you'll look forward to receiving that report.

While getting your own letters is **cool**, writing letters can be a real **nightmare**. How do you start it? How do you sign it off? Worst of all, **what do you say?** How many times have you filled letters with 'very very verys' and lists of things just so you could fill up the page?

If you spend five minutes **Mind Mapping** your letter first, you'll find the letter almost writes itself. You will have **so many ideas** your problem will no longer be filling the page; it will be keeping down the number of pages you write.

Writing a letter is like writing an essay. (Remember the essay-writing exercise in Chapter Two, page 27?) You **use the Mind Map** to **plan out** exactly what you are going to write and then let your brain and the Mind Map take care of matters for you.

Take a look at the example of a letter-writing Mind Map on pages 110–11 and the letter that was written from it on page 109. Are you ready to do one of your own?

Letters begin!

★ To Mind Map a letter, you **start by drawing a picture in the middle**. Then draw **branches** coming off it for all of the main ideas.

★ *Who is your letter going to?* *You need to start your letter with the right greeting and sign it off properly. You can use a Mind Map to work out whether these should be* **formal**, *for someone you don't know, or* **informal**, *for friends and family. Take a branch to work out what kind of greeting and sign-off would be most suitable.*

★ *What is the purpose of your letter? In other words, why are you writing it? Use another branch to map out your purpose. This comes in very handy for writing your first paragraph, or introduction.*

★ *Now work on the main body of the letter, between your introduction and your ending. When you are planning* **the content**, *it helps if you think about the* **What–Where–When–Who–Why checkmap** *(page 22). For example:* **What** *are you asking for?* **Where** *will it take place?* **Why?** *Take a branch to work out your content and add further branches coming off this main branch as you think of more details.*

★ *The* **ending** *of the letter should* **round off** *what you have written and* **remind** *you about the purpose of your letter. You can use a main branch coming off the central image to work out your ending. Do this bit last, then you can look at everything you have come up with on the Mind Map to sum up.*

Fun Stuff

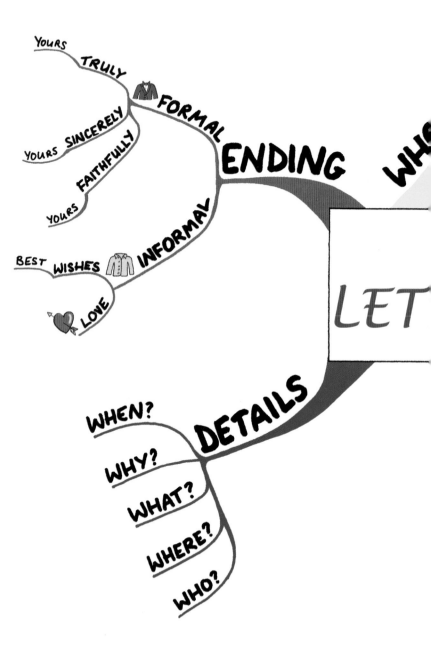

YOURS

TRULY

FORMAL

YOURS SINCERELY

FAITHFULLY

YOURS

ENDING

WHO

INFORMAL

BEST WISHES

LOVE

LET

WHEN?

WHY?

DETAILS

WHAT?

WHERE?

WHO?

GREETING

FORMAL

DEAR SIR
MADAM
MR
MRS

INFORMAL

DEAR NAME

ER

PURPOSE

ASK ?
COMPLAIN
EXPLAIN
DESCRIBE

Five Easy Steps to Writing a Letter

1. Who is your letter to?

2. What greeting do they need?

Formal

Begin with:

Dear Mr/Mrs/Ms
(if you know their name)

Dear Sir/Madam
(if you don't know their name)

End with:

Yours sincerely (if you know their name)

Yours faithfully (if you don't know their name)

Informal

Begin with:

Dear <first name>

End with:

With love from/Best wishes/Love

3. What is the purpose of your letter? Put this in your first paragraph. For example:

★ *Thank someone*
★ *Invite someone to an event*
★ *Complain about something*
★ *Describe something that has happened*
★ *Ask for something*

4. Go into more detail in the main part of the letter. Use the What–Where–When–Who–Why checkmap to help you.

5. Sum up everything in the final paragraph.

Dear Mr Beckham,

I am your absolutely NUMBER ONE, greatest fan. I think you're really shillful and England's greatest player so far. Man U is my favorite team and Dad has promised me tickets to see you play.

I love Victoria's songs and I reckon Brooklyn and Romeo will probably be singing footballers. I'm envious of you and all your family like no-one else.

I would be pleased beyond anything else if you and your family came to my sports day and help us raise money for charity. The date is the 4th of July, on a sunday.

If I can pursuade you, I would be popular plus, have my dreams fulfilled. It would be great if you could come.
yours sincerely,

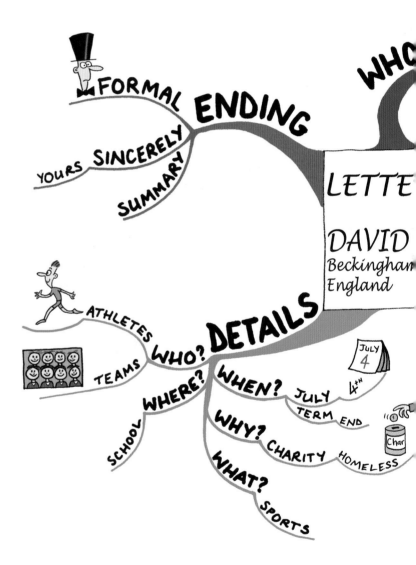

FORMAL ENDING

YOURS SINCERELY

SUMMARY

WHO

LETTE

DAVID
Beckingham
England

ATHLETES

DETAILS

TEAMS

WHO?

WHERE?

WHEN?

JULY
4

JULY 4ᵗʰ

TERM END

SCHOOL

WHY?

CHARITY

HOMELESS

Char

WHAT?

SPORTS

BECKHAM FAMILY
DAVID
VICTORIA
BROOKLYN
ROMEO

TEAMS ENGLAND
MANCHESTER UNITED
FAVOURITE
TICKETS
Ticket

TO
ECKHAM
lace

GREETINGS FORMAL
DEAR MR BECKHAM

PURPOSE INVITATION
SPORTS DAY

We're All Going on a Mind-Mapped Holiday

Not everyone is lucky enough to get to go on holiday, but we can all dream!

Imagine you had as much money as you wanted and could go anywhere in the world (or off the world). What kind of holiday would you plan for yourself? Using the Mind Map on page 114 as an example, Mind Map out your **dream holiday**.

- ★ To start off, draw a **holiday picture** in the middle of the page and label it 'My Dream Holiday'.
- ★ Next, let your **imagination** go wild. Imagine all the possible kinds of holidays there are including: biking, hiking, beaching, sailing, clubbing, slobbing, exploring and special-interest! Think about who you would ideally want with you. Where would be the best place to go? What could be the best time to go?
- ★ Having completed your **magical imagination tour**, select the main branches for your Mind Map and add your key words and images.
- ★ When you have added your main branches, draw some thinner lines from them so that you can add more detail.
- ★ Continue to let your imagination flow free, adding more and more **detail** until you have completed your ideal holiday Mind Map (make sure to take your Mind Map pad and pens with you on that holiday).

Persuading parents
Mind Maps help you present a case that is clear, concise, logical, persuasive and irresistible!

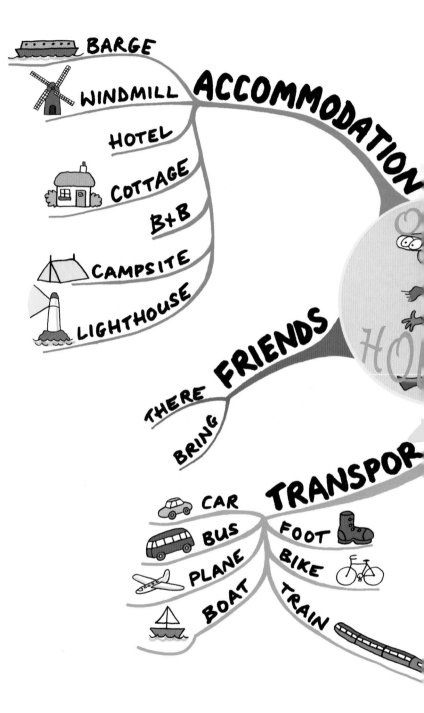

BARGE

WINDMILL

ACCOMMODATION

HOTEL

COTTAGE

B+B

CAMPSITE

LIGHTHOUSE

THERE **FRIENDS**

BRING

HO

TRANSPOR

CAR

BUS FOOT

PLANE BIKE

BOAT TRAIN

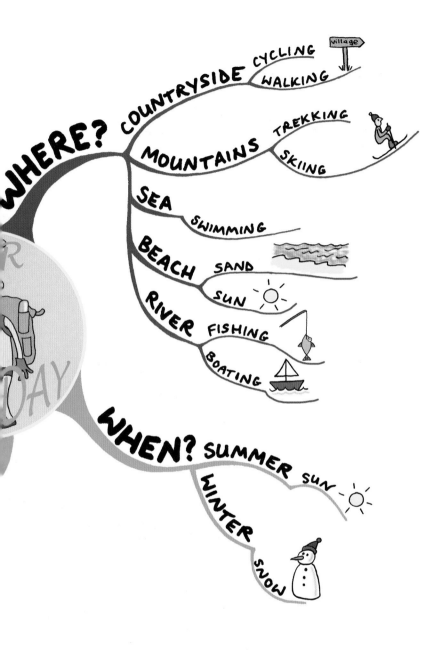

WHERE? COUNTRYSIDE CYCLING
WALKING
village

MOUNTAINS TREKKING
SKIING

SEA
SWIMMING

BEACH SAND
SUN

RIVER FISHING
BOATING

WHEN? SUMMER SUN

WINTER SNOW

Mind Maps for Ever

Please send me any of your most brilliant Mind Maps and your stories of success – there will be many!

Congratulations! You now know the **secret formula** that can put you ahead of the rest – **Mind Maps!** Apply this formula to your schoolwork and you will have everyone wondering exactly what your secret is as you get **better grades** and do your homework in **half the time.**

The Mind Maps you have learnt to use are a **tool** as powerful as any magic wand.

Mind Maps will be your friends for the rest of your life, and will help you, as you now know, to remember better, to solve problems, to concentrate, to be less stressed, to amaze your teachers, ace your exams and impress your friends. You know how brilliant **Mind Maps** (and you!) can be.

You are joining a growing club of millions of people around the world who are using Mind Maps to make them successful.

You now possess the secret formula that will keep you ahead in every situation. With Mind Maps up your sleeve, you can go out and make the most of your **brainpower** and **get the grades** – and the life – you deserve.

BUZAN CENTRES

For information on all Buzan products and courses:
email: Buzan@BuzanCentres.com
website: www.BuzanCentres.com

UK:
Buzan Centre Ltd Headquarters
54 Parkstone Road
Poole
Dorset BH15 2PG

Tel: +44 (0) 1202 674676
Fax: +44 (0) 1202 674776

USA:
Buzan Centre USA Inc. (Americas)
P.O. Box 4
Palm Beach
Florida 33480

Free Toll in USA +1 866 896 1024
USA +1 734 207 5287

Make the most of your mind today

Index

Mind Maps for Kids

Fun Stuff

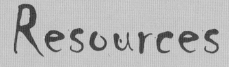

Resources

Make the most of your mind today!

You can now make fantastic Mind Maps on your computer thanks to a brilliant new interactive Mind Map programme called iMindMap™. For your free 30-day trial of iMindMap visit **www.BuzanMindMap.com** and follow the instructions online.